PENELOPE IN FIRST PERSON

SUE GOYETTE

PENELOPE

in first person

———————

GASPEREAU PRESS LIMITED

PRINTERS & PUBLISHERS

2017

Amid weird collisions of feeling

and gladioli, first and foremost, I want

to thank my dearest adversary for

putting a fire up under my words, for

releasing my husband when a stunned

fish emerged from an aqueous pit,

spit on his hands, and threw his old

house out the window.

C.D. WRIGHT, FROM «SOME OLD
WORDS WERE SPOKEN»

How much feeling can there be?
A lot.
The branches of my heart they pulse and stop.
And start.

VEDA HILLE, FROM «THE TREES»

I wake to visitors at the door. Can we get something
to drink? I'm asked. Dutifully, I call for more chairs.

Can we get something a little stronger? they say. They say,
can you make us a sandwich while you're up? Trees are felled

in the south lot for more chairs. The care dutifully given
to joints and spindles sacrificed, the carpenters forced

to assemble rudimentary stools then boxes. Constrained by
protocol, I count the visitors silently but they are that jammed in,

I lose track of their legs. By week's end, the demand to be seated
so unruly, the carpenters are delivering stumps, then entire logs.

9

I wake confused. It's noon somewhere, right?
I'm asked. The visitors? I reply. Just fell asleep,

I'm told. Are you really going to start a band?
I'm asked. My recall, initially, is dutiful.

Was it so terrible that I had sung? But then my ears
feel the first scalloping heat of chagrin. Its warmth

spreads as proclamations and boasts return to roost,
shrill and pleased with themselves. How had I got up

on the table and whose hat had I worn? Loss tends
to its fires patiently. The shame I feel burns like paper.

The weeks wake to months. Years. Can we get another table
in the beer tent? I'm asked. There's a beer tent? I reply. I'm flustered.

And I'm drunk. The visitors are potent compliments. They've never seen
a better spoon, tasted better brew. Our harbour, according to them,

is the finest they've laid eyes on. Each stone in its proper
place, how had I come up with that? My cup is kept proficiently

filled. And my tongue rallies back. I banter, I cajole. I screech
the crooked logic women know when our hearts are aghast and silenced.

I tend to the visitors with appalling decorum. They cheer me on,
so I blow. I blow. Odysseus's candle sputters then quits. I did that.

I wake to dread. I banish questions
so I can think. My dignity has been plucked.

My dignity, pink-puckered and overexposed. My mouth
lined in ash. The fire, started in revelry, has passed out.

If I had tarted up my loneliness, if I am to claim my dark ripeness,
I am now left craven to my own needs. The poison I taste

is personal. My mouth abhors me and I abhor
my mouth. If I had the energy to cut myself without mess,

without bother, I would. And if Odysseus is a candle, who is
the match? Not me. I am no longer to be trusted near open flame.

I wake to a swarm of suitors
and though everyone insists they're harmless as trees,

I can feel them leering. Is that not a forest?
I'm asked. Then why are there so many

tongues? I reply. I dress dutifully,
see to the clover and rabbits but as soon as my back

is turned, the trees move closer. At first axe swing,
my wrist complains and my shoulder grieves.

If I know anything, it's about loss. My blade
will need sharpening before nightfall.

I wake to their version. My suitors
are eager. Is this not a lark? I'm asked.

Why aren't there more guards? I reply
I dress dutifully and adjust my belt

but once dressed, feel too trousseau-ed.
My women help with the buckles.

At first, the quill is all feather and my request
keens for flight. If I know anything, it's about

diplomacy. The ink holds my future. With a careful hand,
I soften my demand. *Please,* I begin, by furling.

I wake to rabbit. My husband is away
and the rabbit's ear the original receiver. Is this not

the future? I'm asked. Have I not pressed my mouth
to its suede, whispering an intimate wind for my husband's return?

I reply. I dress dutifully, my body a bent mast
looking for my other shoe. The "forest" tries to distract me

but its "trees" grow with such swagger, my own sap blushes. If I know
nature, it's about loss. *You promised*, I hiss, piercing

their leaves to branches with my needle. The industry of my anger
has the forest sewn by nightfall. Autumn I'll learn of the hard way.

I wake to a vision of Odysseus bearing
two cups of wine. Are you not thirsty? I'm asked.

Can you not come back for real? I reply. I dress dutifully
but add petals to my underthings. These petals

are another form of request. The age without
husband may allow birdsong to alight these petals

into sweet tongues. If I know desire, it's losing
its heat but will flare an impatient need

when I try fanning it out. If anything, my legs have tongue
burns that are haunting me of a matrimonial feast.

I wake to a longing more private
than husband. Is this the original vow? I ask.

Its new land has unfamiliar customs and is bare
of company. I watch my breath roll as far as it

can before igniting to eelgrass. I dress
dutifully as a landowner, finessing that ownership

with bootstraps and a walking stick: kindling for this new
enterprise. If I am to reacquaint with fire, it will be as fireweed.

When I bend to test the apricots, the vendor whispers:
but how will you speak anything tender with such flames?

I wake to my son just getting home. Will you
leave me alone, I'm asked. Why is your voice

so gristled? I reply. My boy has manifested thorns
and pierced himself with authority. He smells of roast

meat and sacrifice. I dress my wound dutifully,
cursing myself for weaving my version but not

including his. A new voice in the choir of mothers at their windows
watching a strange boat peel out of the harbour. If I know family,

it's about loss. One side of my bed weighted by empty,
my table set for three: the chime of chairs, quivering.

I wake to trees. Didn't you see the guards? I ask.
Is that what they are? they reply, crunching. Up close,

I understand they've bred with my dreams and know my
secrets. I vow not to marry any of them and throw

my book at the closest maple. *Ironic*, it flirts. Pulp and Paper,
their new pet name for my struggle. I dutifully dress

my voice with subtlety. My breathing is spent of flames
so smoke is all I'm capable of. If I know safety, it's about

danger. My smoke takes a ferocious shape, but then whittles
and is wanting. The trees, fluent in fire, can really feel me, they say.

I wake to the future. My husband will come home
with reasons crammed into excuses. Weren't the days just pelts

without me? I'll be asked. But what did you do with their eyes?
I'll reply and at once the ghosts of the animals will appear

wreaking havoc on our marriage. I'll learn of snort
and hoof and use those tactics throughout our couple

counselling. I'll dress dutifully though my body will
push at the seams. My stature will have changed but weeks

will go by before my husband will notice. If I know aging,
it too is about loss, unrolling its heroic greeting forward.

I wake to another day. Are you not bored
of scanning the horizon? I'm asked. Did I ask you?

I reply. My noble son has exhaled so much smoke
I have a different landscape on my hands. Exposed

rabbits are too easy to hunt, I announce to the suitors
who've asked to see my pelt. I dress dutifully

in furs nonetheless, relishing the soft seduction cuffed to my
wrists. My son has smoked most of the furniture

and my husband's hunting clothes. If I know havoc,
it's the loss it has wreaked. Where are my keys? I bellow.

I wake hungover, my sullen tongue a warp in dried weft.
Are you alone? I was asked. Do you see anyone else?

I had replied. The lighting was poor and it had taken
a few tumblers to realize I was drinking with wolves.

I had dressed dutifully but was now alarmed
at the bounty of rabbit fur adorning me. When our server

informed us the kitchen was closed, I had gulped
secretly, fogging my composure. If I knew anything,

it was about loss not about self-defence, though when I vowed
to tear the wolves into limbs I felt a goddess stirring.

I wake to goddess. Where did you get these?
I'm asked. They were a gift from Odysseus, I reply.

The goddess winds the strand under her breasts
then hovers up to taste the chandelier. She lowers

only to undo the duty by which I've dressed,
unzipping a floor-length rage that will one day be the rage.

Funny how anger can be so ancient and so modern, the goddess
muses. If I know rage, it's about smoldering

but once the goddess tells me about Circe, I truly lose
my shit. And he'll fall for it? I shrill, *for how many years?*

I wake up mortal. Would you like us to let out
the waist, I'm asked. Let out the *what*? I reply.

I march down to the harbour and address
the sea. The sea listens then erodes my rage

with its *feeling a little perimenopausal?* smirk. I threaten
to chew up fishing nets and cough up their knots.

I'll unscrew the big light bulb and watch flowers
wither. Middle finger up, the goddess coaches.

If I know the shore, it's about low tide. Which boat can we send?
I say, holding the sea so close I can see up its clamshells.

I wake to a plan. What if you catch a creature?
I'm asked. All the better to eat you, I reply, pulling

my weaving to the shore. I dress the ocean dutifully,
my net settling like a second skin. I consult the elders

and they suggest word games to keep my brain
nimble. Speaking at length into a rabbit's ear, I grow irritated

by its tremor. I take the time to really pluck every last dastardly whisker
from my chin. The bell rings when my net catches a young boy

and his cigarettes. If I know anything, it's how loss
is using us as bait. Heh, heh, mimics the sea with its waves.

I wake to the same day. I'm asked, I reply.
I dress dutifully. If I know anything about loss

it's about loss. I hurt my toe kicking at swagger so limp back
to my room to brood. My suitors are coming

to a boil and if I don't stir them constantly, they'll harden.
Fuck my suitors, I say to the mirror, looking past my reflection

to get at my future. The suitors outside my door mistake my anger
for passion and pass the *fuck my suitors* around like an amuse-bouche,

savouring how the meaty 'fuck' spices the 'my' and oils them, my suitors.
Is it getting hot in here? they jostle, preening into the keyhole.

I wake to a hot breath that disrupts the other morning sounds.
How do you like me now? I'm asked, an ongoing monologue,

studded. Let's get out of these wet clothes, they say, licking their sleeve.
As out of hand as the suitors have grown, my replies remain demur,

distracting, or I change the subject. When I say: what are your plans today?
or: is your family asking after you? their voice increases in debauchery.

Let me show you what I've got planned, they say. I listen dutifully
while reckoning privately with my old flap of fear and dread.

If my silence knows loss, it's sweetened by a hard candy that sounds
soft at first, then ennobles itself to a much bigger and billowing: ENOUGH.

I wake to a horse. Are you in my dream? I'm asked.
Do I look like a dream? I reply. Were we just pillaging

a castle but didn't take the gold? I'm asked. I would never
take anyone else's gold, I reply. Was there a goddess

who spoke as an owl, commanding us to leave
by way of the river? I'm asked. Was she wearing a long string

of pearls under her breasts? I reply. Are you the lady
who's been waiting for a husband for a pathetically long time?

I'm asked. Are you fucking kidding me? I reply. The horse
and I study each other until our edges meld, our forces join.

I wake as a horse. Do you agree to return when I say?
I'm asked. I'll neigh once for yes, I reply.

The other horse instructs me how to gallop over great distances:
with an easy compliment, kissing both cheeks. I feel my muscles

rumble on like a furnace, heat rising through new vents. Ah, now
I understand nostrils for this need to flare. Soon, I'm in a field

of sheep looking for my husband, and then there he is, atop a woman
with flowing hair, a waist so slim it barely makes biological sense.

My hoofs are invented then to punctuate this information.
When I dutifully, womanly, stomp, loss migrates to animal, braying.

I wake in a field. What am I to do? I ask.
All four legs require unfolding, an impulse verging

on reply, so I dutifully get up. The morning, a small
patch of bitter grass and niblets of clover, entices me. My teeth

work with such economy, I test their design by chomping.
Wild strawberries greet me by imploding sweetness in the salad

I'm composing. I move from stalk to scrub to clump.
If I know anything, it's loss, but maybe loss is a receding illness

I have endured. If it's chronic, another symptom may be small moans
and the thrust of my husband's hips. A new version of cough and fever.

I wake enraged in horse-form. Do you feel like
stampeding? I'm asked. Is there something more

painful? I reply. I dutifully behead clover and mince
grass to juice. I piss freely, I shit, but then I nick

my confidence by checking myself in the mirror. The goddess
stirs the lake and insists I'm still a glossy chestnut. My snort

is practiced. I hoof the earth to stir up dust. Stampede isn't
big enough. I'll come down on his body with such force he'll be

puddled. I'll hold my hoof over the woman's eyes and ask
how she's feeling now. It's time to go, I'm told. Firmly.

I wake to loss. Do you miss the horse? I'm asked.
Can you make me ferocious? I reply. The goddess brushes the hair

from my face and, before dressing me for my duties,
washes me. Each limb held with such delicacy,

I weep. My bath becomes my broth and I drink
of myself to remember my good marrow. The goddess folds each

of my fingers into fist then puts it to her mouth. When the goddess
breathes on my fists, embers in my heart inflate to flame.

What is this taste? the goddess asks. She holds my hand
and licks. Briefly, mercifully, she dulls the glare.

I wake to silence. Are you ready? I'm asked.
I undress dutifully is my reply. My mirror studies me,

examining the soft folds that hold my shame. The years mapped
in the terrain of stretch marks and slur, pucker and pouch.

I'm rooted so deeply in this myth that when my marriage
fails, it will stain my son, my name. My legs are thin

but bold. I flex my calf to measure its muscle. What I behold
of loss lives in my body and everything about myself

is homesick. Is this mortality? I hold to a luxuriant pace, the oil
of jasmine and orange bowing to animal before anointing me back.

I wake to dripping. Are you awake? I'm asked.
Are you the ceiling? I reply. The ceiling sighs. I loathe that name,

it complains. How may I address you? I say dutifully.
What about Gateway to the Heavens? Or Better Than Floor?

What's dripping? I ask. Your Vat of Tears is leaking, Gateway
to the Heavens informs me. Someone sloshed into it and rendered a hole.

If I know anything it's about salt water and this new tide of tears
isn't the concern it would've been before seeing my husband "plowing

his field". Are my tears escaping or being re-wept? I ask. Some are
escaping but some are definitely re-crying, is Better Than Floor's guess.

I wake to a change of heart. You will no longer
bathe your husband in the tears you shed while he was lost

at sea? I'm asked. Lost at "sea"? I reply. Dutifully, I had thought
immersing him in my own salt water would properly wash him

of the danger he'd faced while he marinated tender
in my love, but I'd rather braise him now than marinate him.

Bring me a bottle, I say. He can drink my tears
if he's thirsty for the truth. I know loss so well,

I'm ready to lose everything and at the very least I'll be left
with a bottle. Make it a jug, my nimble mind insists.

I wake as rabbit. Are you ready to hear his side?
I'm asked. My rabbit heart, so closely related

to land mine, implodes rather than replying. The goddess
waits dutifully, dressing her voice with violets she picked

for my dream. And the white stone she'd brought
from the far shore is thrown now, rippling the day and obscuring

its clock. I give him my ear and, at first, hear nothing.
After the smoke clears, I can hear the heat of his mouth, how his breath

still maintains its alert compass for home. If I know anything,
it's the loss of hearing him say my name, but now I hear him breathe it.

I wake. Where are you? I'm asked. I don't
know, I reply. Do you have fur? I check with my nose

and smell dry earth, beneath thirst, a scalp.
I don't know. My breasts are still dutiful headstones. I must be

a mother. To who? I'm asked. I root the lair for clues.
The bones I find are pens or maybe small weapons.

A fire had burned but has been neglected and is now bitter, goitered
by rocks. I taste the ash and remember a bed. I taste

the coal and remember a tongue. I must be in a marriage, I say.
I hit my head on its low ceiling, I mean on its low Better than Floor.

I don't wake. Do you need another violet? I'm asked.
The river is swallowing them like candy, I reply. And another

violet appears long enough for my foot to find it. In this way,
I'm crossing over. My suitors, on the backshore, are leering:

cupcake, pudding, tenderloin, they beckon, their lusty voices
soon snatched by hawks. Dutifully, I'm exploring my options. Each violet

a step forward. The goddess keeps her supply fresh. When my foot bruises
a flower, I'm renewed by the soft purple sigh of wilt. When the next

shore appears, I have to agree to eat only what I need. Some flowers
know nothing of loss and will gasp out loud when plucked.

I wake surrounded by blossoms. Can you be bird? I'm asked
How? I reply. My shoulders bellow trumpets of feathers.

My spine fans the downward reach of a navigational rudder. Dutifully
I flap to swoop then glide. Oh, I say, undressed. We rest

on thermals, sleeping in our hulls, our wings, steady oars
keeping us aloft. I flail only when I wonder what time it is,

I sink only when I think of my son. The goddess throws a blue
stone and my sky clears of clouds. When I think of telling

Odysseus, my shoulders strengthen and life courses through me.
If I know anything, this version of loss feels more like erupting.

The suitors outside Penelope's door wait for her to wake.
They buck for a sweet spot where they'll be lit but also

in shadow. Mysterious yet fetching. Some have shaved,
grooming their hair dutifully. Rutting in the waft of her pale

perfume, her plume for so long, some are smeared in grease.
Those meditating on her beauty test gourmet words for her wrists,

her ankles. The suitors who can smell her bed feel their cocks
firework into more expansive versions of cock; even their ears

cock. If the door knows anything, it's about hinges,
how a homecoming would be easier on them than this sideshow.

.

The door wakes to the suitors talking to it. And the door
is smitten. Do you want a piece of this? it's asked.

The door has no idea how to respond. Dutifully it feels its planks
line up. Occasionally, it has visions of a verdant pushing

or pulsing that tastes green. It aches before a rain. This ache
rusts its bores. If its keyhole is a dialect of 'yes', it's also

a one-sided argument for 'no.' It connoisseurs the grips on its latch,
can feel the soul of each suitor's intent. Few understand how iron

is a slow version of tongue. If these suitors taste of anything,
it's sweat and meat, renewing the door's loyalty for its locks.

I wake to flowers. We need to talk, I'm told.
You're all leaf, they say. Boring, says one voice. Necessary,

says another. The voices are perfume, sweet
and light but careful. They land on my skin

and melt. Warnings or kisses, I can't decide.
You're not listening, they say. Critics, maybe. The mingling

of scent, the perfect roar of petals, their insistence makes me
dizzy. If I know anything, I can barely believe the zinnia

and want to bleed the thick grief keeping me quiet.
Loss isn't a wound, I'm told, it's the slit from which I'll bloom.

I wake transformed. Do you mind bee-tickle?
I'm asked. Do you mind the stretch?

Do you remember how thwarted you felt? Are you
getting used to your new throat? That ruffle suits you.

How are your tendrils blazing? Have you tried hollowing?
The moment where tongue meets nectar is an early state

of bliss. Relax beauty, you keep house carelessly. Is there
a word for this weeping? And for this extending,

for the pushing into finale? Into arrival? And then wilt again?
Exhaustion/exaltation? Oh, petal goddess, welcome. Finally.

Telemachus wakes hungry. Do you want your blue tunic
or your green one? he's asked. Where's my mother?

he replies. The shrug is spiced with unpleasant implication.
What? he says. The shrug is smug. Its secret blade

toys with the satin lining of his mother's reputation.
Telemachus is of oak therefore stubborn and not given

to flight. More rooted, he pounds the kinship of table. The shrug
doesn't have enough fawn blood for his liking. It is too

raccoon, too carry-on-eating, what-are-you-going-to-do-about-it?
He takes his knife to the shrug but its pit just laughs at him.

Telemachus wakes without his mother. On a scale of one
to ten, how angry are we feeling today? he is asked. Where is

my mother, he replies. He is volcanic, he's told. He has dressed
for war but, look, all they're having is tea. Maybe

some buns. His voice meddles with his jawbone, rewires
his tongue and stands back before careening up the lonely

tunnel. His voice may be lava but is taking the horses with it. The shrug
shrugs so his bones bend, undo their clasps, and stretch. Get that cobweb

while you're up there, he is told. The day Telemachus becomes a man
is the day, across leagues of sea and field, his father eats some charred mutton.

Telemachus wakes in thunder. Aren't you supposed to be volcanic?
he's asked. He lets them simper before storming. His lightening

is proficient, following his arterial anger with a cursive flare
for a target. The suitors. Their shrugs. They try placating him with song

only to learn that a song will burn at chorus first before sizzling
the rest of its lyrics like bacon. Yum, Telemachus says, eating

anything they offer. You're ruining everything, they say.
You're nothing like your father, they say. It will be remembered

as a dark day, the day Telemachus took things into his own hands.
He'd eat their ruin and tell their shades they tasted like chicken. Oh.

The door wakes to Telemachus. Let me in, it's told.
Its lock is diplomatic until attacked then will dutifully hold

to its bolts. Telemachus's shoulder tastes of boy
but his breath is loose with something amateurly hinged.

The door has been a surrogate father to the boy and understands
the lightening to be his personal threshold of pain. Shh, the door

nurses. It softens its wood for the boy's shoulder. This time,
he won't bruise. This time he'll recognize the door for the wood

he had whispered into. Up close, the door releases a waft of childhood
words the boy once breathed. A thankless job it does with utter devotion.

Telemachus wakes locked out of his dream. Am I to pick up
the sword before it turns to flower? he asks it. Or am I to leave

the flower in the ground to sweeten the earth for my father's
bones? When my father said: get a horse, did he mean a horse

or was he telling me to come to my senses and saddle a confidence
I've been lacking? Is my mother the swan or is she the sword?

Wait, is she the flower? If my mother is the flower and my father
the old stable hand, who am I? Am I the hen? Maybe I'm the egg?

Then why was I sitting on the shore before a boat laden with salt?
Was that why I was crying? Why am I always the one crying?

The goddess wakes beside a flower. Is it time to return?
she is asked. Is your tongue stamen or stigma? she replies.

The stamen is many tongues, the flower dutifully recites.
Botany, both goddess and flower besmirch. This zinnia is

the deepest pink with a craving for orange. The moonlight
powdered onto its style wafts mystery. Its ovary is its kitchen stove

and its hips, early in the progress of fruiting. Thinking
of a husband wilts its leaves. Each thought of a child

costs it some colour. If it knows anything, it's the pale
price to love them. All the pink it still needs to spend.

I wake to a flower. Are you now the goddess?
I'm asked. Are you now the transformed? I reply.

If I am the goddess, I decide to be taller,
to measure my stride by province. I compose more

elaborate clouds for the lonely and mother the single
elms with sheep. By the way I nectar a dream of Odysseus

and I at the easy task of picking peaches, I know
forgiveness. For us, I give weight to low branches with fruit,

dappling our talk with laughter. I know him that well, he'll will
himself to sleep so he can finally taste what he's been craving.

Odysseus wakes to the idea of home. Is it my walls or my fields
you're missing? he's asked. It's the way she sat then pushed

closer to me unbeckoned, he replies then dutifully whets his
composure and dulls his sword on small talk. Each of his feet have a turn

in his hands. He speaks to them as animals, giving them the simple
command: *home.* This command shares a wall with prayer. Both

of the same house with different closets. If he knows anything, it's about
the passing of time. He knows of minutes, then hours, days, weeks, months.

And years. His tongue worries now at the nub of a new word. He tests it
out loud in his solitude then shudders. What is this thing: *decades*?

I wake with a piece of string in my hand. Should you be addressed
as goddess? I'm asked. What happens if I pull? I reply.

The string gives just enough resistance to make the pulling
interesting. I dutifully use just a finger and thumb.

It's a delicate if not complicated act. I feel a florid implication
arise and then settle. I feel a tidal shift and a high wind. I feel

birds pause, mid-flight and curious at the sudden distinction
in green. Some fish, accustomed to this lure, pull back. Destined

to plates, fate begins as hooks in their mouths. And Odysseus,
bent to lace his shoes, now he stands to take his leave.

The bed wakes to Penelope. Hold me closer, it is told.
The bed softens its regard and fleshes itself vulnerable.

It is a master of comfort having studied with the great
gurus of service and esteem. It offers itself like a tongue,

inviting her body to dissolve like sugar while her spirit spins.
In this way, it's flavoured by the unexpected fluency

of beasts chasing tables and candles lit in its branches. The bed knows
this woman like the back of its hand. It has been chosen for its ability

to weigh the girth of her tears with the small scales of its pillows.
It starts out cold so it can grow a warmth specific for her.

I wake with a mission. For this decluttering, will you need
containers or crates? I'm asked. Maybe something with bars,

I reply, and padlocks. And what is it you're getting rid of?
I'm asked. Anything that doesn't bring me joy, I reply.

Even my water jug is aghast and wishes it had something carved
into its belly, a bluebell or a dove instead of its clay hips and lippy

handle. The candles rue their smoke stains. The chairs,
their angle. I dutifully pause, if joy is almost extinct,

its migration path still gleams faintly. And if I know loss, I must have,
at some point, known the exuberance of white wings, its trumpet call.

The suitors wake to me. Is this all of you? I ask. How many more can you
handle? they rooster. Your legs are one holy pair of scissors, they say.

Your hair's been licked by the sun, they say,
are you sure you're not a goddess? Mmm girl, I bet you taste

as good as you look. Though my patience is dutiful,
it sometimes pulls on its leash. There'd be no stopping that ass,

I'm told. Smile, I'm told. Show me your tits. My patience
could use a bowl of water—when the suitors finally stop,

I can hear it panting. If I know anything, I say, it's that you don't
give me joy. Come here, Penny, I'll give you joy, they chortle.

The cells wake to suitors. Are they spicy enough? they're asked.
The cells taste the exhaust of them. Not even close, they reply.

Someone throws water on the suitors. To cool them down.
The suitors are a peacock of protest, muddling into each other.

They agree on a *what the fuck* chorus but the cells refuse
to communicate. They've been forged in the deepest fire, trained

in martial silence, and are direct descendants of death. The suitors dent
their shoulders, flex dutifully, then dent themselves again. The cells know

imprisonment is a process. First the suitors will feel protected, having agreed
Penelope is batshit crazy. But then they'll fester, pepper delectably.

Telemachus wakes to a ruckus. Do you still wear these?
he's asked. What are you doing? he replies. Cleaning,

his mother tells him. Where were you? He fights the young
weed in his voice to submission. Where the fuck were you?

he matures, dutifully cinching into his new aftershave. His mother
sits on his bed. She has missed him and there's so much

to say. He marvels how her voice, her proximity, goes from
rub to polish. He fights against the shine and then feels himself

surrender. If he knows anything, it was once how to radiate
before smoke clogged his glow and loss blinded his eyes.

The grand rooms wake to space. Do you remember how to
breathe? they're asked. They extol honey-hearted swifts

as a soft, raptured reply. Their enthusiasm is the informal
invention of decorum and welcome. The grand host of rooms

pushes past corners, exalting walls into the grassy knolls
and marsh outside. Gentle commands are heeded by feathers

plumping ghost birds in the pillows. The fire in the grate
agrees to counsel all who approach so they'll feel a deep numinous

understanding. If these rooms know anything, it's how to relieve
a traveller of her map, give the thirsty a goblet to tend.

I wake to a clean mirror. Have you ever seen
anything so precious? I'm asked. I lean in closer

to study the lines around my mouth, the patch of winter
above my ears. For all I've had to heat, I presume, my hair has snowed.

Criticism's snare loosens its grip and my thoughts are now
unfettered, free to regain their composure. I dutifully

look at my profile and try seeing myself from behind.
Who is this new stranger? I marvel, and what big hips you have.

All the better for you to watch me go, I rehearse. If I know anything,
I'm beginning to realize, it's best to know I know nothing at all.

I wake to the goddess. Can I have these? I'm asked
and watch my jewels bedazzle her fingers.

I'm dutifully lost. The horse I'd been, the bird,
the flower, are faint prints in dream dust. Every night,

I take up their trail but find myself at strange harbours
or thick woods, alone and without hooves or petals to guide me.

When I test my arm, it tastes of yesterday, unmoored
and drifting. When I smell my hair, I find it longing

for smoke. The goddess lights a candle and blows it out. Such industry
it takes you people to stay lit with your fires, she commiserates.

I wake pale. Would chamomile help? I'm asked.
My voice is past fruit. My stalk dry. Is it the matronly season?

I reply, but no one hears me. They move past me as if I'm not
sitting at my table, cutting into my pear. They speak as if my ears

aren't empty teacups. I dutifully keep company with my windows
but even they've grown lazy thinking I'm elsewhere. On a good day,

they offer a glimpse of pine or the tail end of hawk. Mostly
it's the grass blades of the passing field. If I know anything,

it's how to keep busy. In this scrubbed silence, I hear
something else in my nest, how it's brooding on empty.

I wake without a name. There are no questions
or maelstrom of replies. I apply myself dutifully

to the quandary. The leaves I've sewn in place have twisted
their torn selves off the trees and are past ragged,

past being past, and dissolving. My dreams are in canning jars,
bright fruit peeled but browning in night's cellar. This new habitat

is harshest on my voice, offering little to nothing of flavour.
I try the bird's trick of running lightly across my days, forcing

my footsteps to resemble rainfall but the life crammed beneath the hours
stays there. My empty jewel box is just another small casket.

My marriage wakes without a wife. Without a wife there are no
curves and therefore no question marks. Without a wife

no one attends the fertile silence plowed and ready for reply.
Without a wife, breasts seem a new art that endow a shadow

with surplus. The blood on the legs is old syrup from last
year's spring. The days, a series of meals evoking more

meals dutifully. The clock is watched. The chair pulled out.
The plate scraped. All of these actions grow talons to hunt

more actions. The words from the vows refuse voice. The vows
try singing but their ears hear nothing but throat-clearing.

I awake, I woke   am asked

reply and say:

(dutifullydutifullydutifullydutifullydutifully)

if anything
my loss is mortal and has been acting like a goddess.

The horse wakes the hound. The hound wakes the command.
The command wakes the voice. Before the voice wakes the name,

I clean my final house. I begin by stripping the bed
of my swimming sex. I scour the night of its stories.

I dip my cloth in vinegar and take to the mirrors.
There'd be no demur ghosts, no accord stained in a comely

fashion. I dip my hairbrush, my lipstick in the sea.
I release duty to the woods and briefly grieve its spindly legs,

its fey cheer. The shades have fangs it won't be able to converse with.
I sweep the hearth then I straighten, grief on the fire smokes blue.

My name wakes to a voice calling it like a hound.
It startles upright and bounds the glorious run

homeward. My name can feel its paws hit
an easy stride. It catches the scent of sweet neck

and throat: its familiar tunnel. Blood begins to course its veins,
up the staircase of ribs, to its heart. Another homecoming.

A voice calls and my name hounds, snout low
to grass and clover, startling rabbits. My name is beside

itself at being claimed, called back from stale silence, set loose
from rope, from tricks, wagging like there's no tomorrow.

My tongue wakes to a new spice. Not as sweet as before,
is it? I'm asked. I rub the taste into the roof of my mouth,

dig into the deep wells of my teeth for the respite
of familiar taste. My tongue tests along my lips

before my mouth parts. This isn't a wound
but another slit so I may blossom. My voice surprises

me by skating. No, not skating but sliding. My name
skids past all the names, all the words said at me,

gliding with a speed that is unnerving. If everyone is stunned
it isn't because I speak, it's how my name comes out singing.

The feast wakes in a house. How many plates do you have?
it asks. Can we get more chairs? It rubs its hands. It is up

to its ears in plans. It will need candles and better views.
It will push cushions closer together and syrup the affair

with delectable conversation. There'll be music but not too intrusive:
an acoustic creek maybe, a wild phlox choral, or a foxglove aria,

an allium of silence breezed by hummingbirds and the folded
surprise of herons. The feast has delectable ideas that extend onto trays

of aperitifs and bite-size salted things. Art begins to thrum on the walls.
The house turns up a few degrees, warms itself into a home.

Telemachus wakes to music. Is he home, has he come home?
He splurges all his hope and takes to the stairs. The polish

is astounding, the old wood has wakened the flourish of branches
in summer. The table is a glorious heap. And there's his mother,

eating pie. This stops him. Has he ever seen his mother eat pie?
His mother slices pie, she serves it. She knows to push dough

back into itself and roll it flat. Later, it's the pie he'll remember,
cream whipped to an impossible peak and his mother's fork

slicing him a bite. Is he home? he finally manages. What? his mother
says. Odysseus, is he home? No, she says, but there's pie.

I wake in bed after a delightful evening. My bed
still as wide but its wound no longer a sinkhole.

I visit Odysseus's side. His is the view of the harbour
and if I allow my head to swing off the side, my hair

grazing the floor, I can see the moon. His pillow
is still the rural county of his smell. I know three hairs

are beneath it because I found them and placed
them there, a frond I unearth when desperate.

I'll sleep on them tonight. If there are wolves in my dream,
I'll placate them with rabbits. If there's death, I'll greet it.

The suitors fall asleep plotting how they'll plow Odysseus's fields.
They'll water his cows and gather the eggs beneath

the private warmth of his chickens. The private warmth
of his chickens is talk so buxom, so bawdy, it impresses even them

with its cheek. All day, they pace their cells as if this small parcel
of land is just the beginning. They let loose battle cries

to watch them ricochet off the echo of earlier battle cries. Their battle
cries begin to battle each other. Roughnecks of clashing baritones

and bass from throats to hands and legs and teeth. This convergence
of rage and so many eyes resemble a sea monster, rampaging.

Telemachus can't sleep. He has sharpened his father's
memory then his own tongue for the conversations they'll have

when Odysseus does get home. He sharpened his sight for the dreams
he's been having of the relentless creature who bought his scent

from a travelling caravan. He sharpened his fingers so he can dig
deeper into the bullshit the suitors promised him, to finally expose

their pleather. His bed is a griddle, a girdle, a girl. His bed
is a flying saucer. This is his problem: he isn't a disciplined

thinker. His thoughts are without fence and his heart a sulk. How easily
it mopes, tonight his mother taking the bigger piece, then winking.

Only the doors and the cells are awake. They stand their shape
with a mastery that looks deceptively simple. This is when

they show their age. Their bodies lithe but sunken, holding
hard the threshold in the sacred practice of *enter* or *take leave.*

If split apart, their hinges would look arthritic. Overworked knuckles
past their prime and swollen. Their eyes, past seeing, can sense

movement but it's veiled or submerged. They recognize
voice best. The suitors' swag is sawdust, for example. Penelope's voice,

summer's late syrup. And if Telemachus is a young violin,
his voice, the last leafed aria. For him, they open the widest.

One rabbit wakes early. It has perfected its nab for clover,
the sweet stalk a whisker above the horizon, the long tube

of green it minces and then the delectable honey-quilled
flower bursting. The rabbit's ears are trimmed in fur, each bristle

an instrument amplifying any shift in talon, any darkening wing.
Its true ear is pink with topographical lines mapping an ancient

listening, perked to hear the clouds before rain. Or the foot before the sack.
The rabbit is razing a small crop and hearing the pine loosen

a needle. It is hearing a burnt complaint waft between the cook and her pot.
Then the scrape of a hull, but this is faint. The hull of a voyage, a man.

Telemachus wakes to find his endurance has been topped up
by sleep. He'd been given a cup in his dream and was told

to drink. At first, the heat was unbearable but soon steeled
to silver. Upon waking, he'll be invincible for eight hours

and is to test his proficiency carefully. He cuts himself shaving.
He slices into the table long past the apple. The irritation he feels

is maliced by shame but he wrestles it under his chair easily
and when he gets up from the breakfast table, he feels renewed, cleansed

of a boyhood haunt. He stands his height for the first time. When he fights
the sea monster, he holds its tentacles until the writhing stops.

I stay awake to track the tree. I crouch, succumbing
to the cover the shades bequeath. If I have to choose

a colour for the scent of the woods, I can't dismiss the elegant
purple of its edge or its potent spiced rust. To be so delightfully

perplexed is a new joy for me. I kneel to properly view
how each chalice of lichen collects rain for the winged things.

I dare myself a sip, then another. I wait by the tree for a glimpse
of the bird whose voice slides sideways before it trills. The last voice

of my early evenings. The one who's been guiding me to dream.
Gratitude in me is hyacinth. A cluster of bells to peal for this chance.

After the sea monster, Telemachus makes himself a sandwich.
Thick slabs of meat between a plaster of butter on the soft

warmth of fresh bread. His teeth his true army, in formation
now to chew. He orders them open, then closed. They are

obedient, poised for command. The meat puts up a sweet struggle,
resists and then gives over, breaking apart into a victory

so savoury, Telemachus slices some more. He is feeling
good, satiated. All those eyes unlit by him. He stole their sight

for himself. That was clever of him. He pats the pouch. When he ventures
to use this sight, he'll be ready for what he'll see and who he can't.

The shore wakes to an adventure unloading. Would you like me
to widen, it asks, so you can have some time to adjust?

Odysseus is uprooting wild rose bushes in his haste to climb
the overgrown route of his return. He had planned each of these steps

and is now slurping them like hot spoonfuls. Has a man ever been
as famished? The way has steepened and is longer than he remembers.

His wife will be in her room brushing her hair. Or in the kitchen, holding
a bowl of apples she'll drop in her surprise: their reunion to the tune of apples

rolling into corners. His wife—Penelope, he'll be corrected, the wild roses
he had pulled will need replanting. Of course, she is happy to see him.

The dream tries waking me. Why are you still sleeping? it asks.
Look how Telemachus stands next to Laertes in this grove you've greened,

I reply. Look at the shape between them. Doesn't it resemble
Odysseus, his shoulders here above his father's but here beneath

his son's? May I taste the nectar of this emptiness? And how have I remembered
to run with such speed that I'm thirsty again? The dream replies with owl

and, below, Odysseus bent to the labour of climbing. The landscape shifts
and the dream provides an old pine, deeply curved, to land in. The tree knows

loss by the needle but continues to shelter. When the dream lifts its skirt,
a new day emerges, then another. The last days, it seems, of my waiting.

I wake to watch us. What did you do to your hair? we ask.
Our hands fledging, aloft. Nothing, we reply.

Is this the marsh of another dream or us reacquainting with the next
vow? If Odysseus is a mast, am I now a stalk, flowering?

We negotiate the distance between us with awkwardness.
When I tell him of the small hosts of lichen and my sips,

he tastes them. When he speaks the names of his lost men, I hold them
on my tongue until the names wear out their chiming. And when Telemachus

weeps a boy for each year his father has been gone, we open our arms
to welcome them. So many small boys clamouring for family.

"It was just a fling," ███████ *tells me
of* ██████ *'s relationship with* ██████ .
"And," ██ *adds, sounding a little testy,
"only because I was out of town at the time."*

ACKNOWLEDGEMENTS

Dedicated to the Wright-Rainham family.

For the company of lake (& eau de lac), family (Euan!!), my bears
(PSSK), friends, time, poetry (boxes and boxes and boxes of poet-
ry), music, summer moonlight, pines, oaks, cedars, maples, lindens
etc., deep-fried whatever at Seascape (and their rolls!!), Hell's Bay
Brewery, Beyoncé, Joanne & Meghan for their insight and feed-
back, frogs, and frog song, herons, hares, dragonflies, butterflies, spi-
ders, tadpoles, minnows, lake rocks and rushes, multi-storey clouds,
squirrels, the Astor theatre, Gord Downie (*that* Himalayan), Jaws
and real sharks, falling stars/satellites, Carters Beach (sand dollars/
plovers/stretch of), the women who granny-ed me at the hostel and
knit me socks, Maria Bamford (One Big Blob!), Bridget Christie
(buoy*ant*), bare naked trees, the colours pink—really deep pink,
and orange, Veda Hille, C. D. Wright, Leonard Cohen, dusk/lamp-
light, Boulangerie La Vendéenne, Laughing Whale Coffee Roast-
ers, Ted Hutton's vegetables/apples/pears, woodstoves, Gold Star
Bakery, shivering/ice lake view, winter moonlight, snow-bowed
pines, duvets, candlelight, melt & mud, all the dialects of green,
unfurling ferns, tadpoles, baby—on-hind-legs-reaching-for-clover-
baby—hares, hummingbirds, kingfishers, owls, juncos, warblers,
finches, etc., Kaurismäki films, and Pete, I'm so grateful.

Support from the Canada Council for the Arts and Arts Nova
Scotia made the expanse I needed possible.

Thank you to Andrew Steeves and Gary Dunfield at Gaspereau Press for their work and their beautiful books. This one, especially.

Thank you to Carrie Dawson and Dalhousie University's English Department for the Writer-in-Residence opportunity. The experience and the conversations I had continue to invigorate me.

Jessica and Rodney, whoever and wherever you are, I saw your engagement announcement at Carters Beach. We must have just missed each other. It was a beautiful day, the tide just out, the sand perfect for your news. May your epics be joyful and your hearth, warm.

The epigraph from C. D. Wright's poem "Some Old Words Were Spoken," is from the collection *ShallCross* (Copper Canyon Press, 2016). The epigraph from Veda Hille's song "The Trees" is from the CD *This Riot Life* and is used by permission of the artist.

The text of this book was set in a digital revival of MONOTYPE BEMBO, an early twentieth-century book type inspired by letterforms cut by Francesco Griffo in Venice in 1495.

This book was edited and designed by Andrew Steeves and printed offset
and bound under the direction of Gary Dunfield at Gaspereau Press.

7   6   5   4   3   2   1

LIBRARY & ARCHIVES CANADA CATALOGUING IN PUBLICATION

Goyette, Sue, author
    Penelope in the first person / Sue Goyette.
Poems.
ISBN 978-1-55447-174-4 (softcover)
    I. Title.
PS8563.O934P46 2017   C811'.54   C2017-905782-0

GASPEREAU PRESS LIMITED ★ GARY DUNFIELD
& ANDREW STEEVES ★ PRINTERS & PUBLISHERS
47 CHURCH AVENUE, KENTVILLE, NOVA SCOTIA B4N 2M7
Literary Outfitters & Cultural Wilderness Guides

Canada   NOVA SCOTIA